THE IRISH CHAIN QUILT

THE IRISH CHAIN QUILT

Blanche Young
Helen Young Frost

Acknowledgements

Our heartfelt thanks to the wonderful people that helped with this book; Beth Kennedy for her technical advice; Lynette Bingham, Debbie Gordon, Pam Cody, and Steve Hatch for contributing so much to the photography sessions; Laurene Sinema and our friends at the Quilted Apple for their enthusiasm; Brenda Burke for her special sewing tip; Tom Frost and the rest of our families for their support; and, most of all, to all those that generously lent their quilts: Eunice Mahony, Debbie Gordon, Pam Cody, Lynette Bingham, Dalene Thomas, Beth Kennedy, Brenda Werbelow, Mary Andra Holmes, Sandee Streech, Pat Hunt, Louise Brown, Dee Lynn, Ruth Gale, Laurene Sinema, and Audrey Waite.

Published by C&T Publishing, P.O. Box 1456
Lafayette, CA 94549

ISBN: 0-914881-14-0

Contents

Introduction

Supplies _____ 7

Fabrics & Design _____ 8

Making the Quilts _____ 10

Finishing the Quilts _____ 35

Double Irish Chain _____ 38

Triple Irish Chain _____ 42

Quadruple Irish Chain _____ 46

Quilting Designs _____ 49

Applique Designs _____ 56

Introduction

The *Irish Chain* quilt has always been a favorite of ours, and of many other quilters judging by the profusion of quilts of this pattern. It's easy to see why; the design is simple, yet graphic; it can be made in units or blocks; and best of all, it has large background spaces to fill with gorgeous quilting!

The *Irish Chain* is certainly one of the oldest documented quilt patterns. The New York Historical Society has a *Double Irish Chain* quilt that is initialed and dated 1822. *Godey's Lady's Book* mentions the pattern "Irish chain" as early as 1849. How the name originated is not known. We have quilter friends in Ireland that have always referred to the pattern as "American Chain"!

Of course the antique quilts were constructed very differently from the methods we are presenting. The quilter of a hundred years ago cut each square one at a time and then pieced the quilt by hand. Our methods involve the cutting and sewing of strips of fabric instead of individual squares. This is not only easier and faster but allows for greater accuracy on the sewing machine. And since we have been using and teaching this method since 1974, we have lots of tips and ideas to share.

The *Irish Chain* is a marvelously versatile pattern. We have included *Double, Triple* and *Quadruple* variations in wall, baby, and bed size. In the color plates we've featured quilts in many color combinations, and in both traditional and contemporary styles. And we also offer some delightful variations using applique, fabric placement, and borders.

We hope you'll enjoy making your *Irish Chain* quilt as much as you'll enjoy using it!

Supplies

Templates	Templates can be made from posterboard. A grided ruler or plastic strips for quilters can also be used.
Markers	A soft leaded pencil will mark on most fabrics. Use a white chalk pencil for very dark fabrics.
Ruler	You will need a 6 inch or 12 inch ruler and a yard-stick or tape measure.
Scissors	Since several layers of fabric will be cut, a good sharp pair of scissors is necessary.
Rotary Cutter/Mat	Many quilters now prefer rotary cutters over scissors. A special mat and metal straight edge are used with the cutter.
Spray Starch	We find that lightly starching the fabrics helps with every stage of construction.
Thread	Use a good quality thread, matching the lightest color in the quilt.
Sewing Machine	These methods were developed for machine piecing.
Needles	Quilting needles (betweens) in sizes 8, 9, 10 or 12. Baste with sharps or milliners' needles.
Batting	Batting is sold in packages in different weights and sizes. A very thin batting will quilt much better and give a traditional look to the quilt.
Hoops/Frames	Many styles of frames and hoops are available. We prefer using a hoop on a stand.

Fabrics & Design

Fabrics

The traditional *Irish Chain* quilt usually had a white background with one other color, such as red or indigo blue, forming the chains. Or two colors, such as red and green, would form the chain. The fabrics were either solid or a tiny print. Several of the quilts in the color plates achieve a traditional look by following this scheme.

Using printed fabrics will give a more contemporary look. Almost any type of print can be used; florals, geometrics, dots, and paisleys. It's best to avoid stripes and one-way prints, especially for the *Triple* and *Quadruple* variations, because of the way the background block is constructed. We have found that even large prints work well; they give a lacy effect to the design. Prints can also be used as the background fabric. A subtle design such as a dot or sprig will still show off the quilting. Or try a large print, with small prints or solids as the chains for a completely different appearance.

Although most antique examples have a light background, it is possible to use medium or even dark fabrics forming the chain. Usually *Irish Chains* have high contrast between the fabrics. We've experimented with some different approaches such as the subtle blending of colors in *Irish Coffee* in plate 15.

After deciding on the placement of the fabrics, cut a small swatch of each one.

Fabrics should be all cotton or cotton/polyester. Avoid very flimsy or loosely woven fabrics. Sewing will proceed much smoother if all the fabrics used are similar in weight.

Variations

Interest can be added to the quilt by centering a motif in the print as shown in the wall quilt on the back cover. The quilt in plate 13 was made with the design centered in the background block and also in some of the chain squares. The squares can still be treated as strips by connecting them with tape.

Applique is an obvious choice for accenting the quilt. The apples in plate 23 and the hearts in plate 4 were centered in the background block. Designs that extend into the chain block would also be effective.

Types of prints

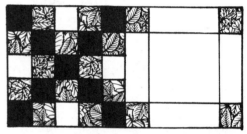

Light background

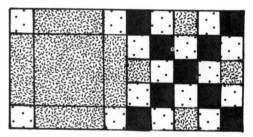

Dark background

Centering a design

Design

Although the *Double Irish Chain* quilt is sometimes referred to as *Triple Irish Chain,* the design is different. Think of each square as a link in a chain. The *Double Irish Chain* does have three squares horizontally but only two squares diagonally. With the center square the same fabric as the background it is easier to see this. The *Triple Irish Chain* has five squares across but the first, third and fifth form the chains. The *Quadruple* variation has seven squares across, with the first, third, fifth, and seventh touching corners and forming the chains.

We've labeled, instead of numbered, the chains for fabric placement. The *Double Irish Chain* has a center chain and two outer chains. The *Triple Irish Chain* has a center chain, two inner chains and two outer chains. The *Quadruple* variation is made with a center chain, two inner chains, two between chains, and two outer chains.

The *Double Irish Chain* quilt can be made with two or three fabrics. The *Triple Irish Chain* can be made with two, three, or four fabrics. The *Quadruple* variation utilizes up to five fabrics. Yardage amounts are listed separately for each chain. Just combine the amounts when using the same fabric for different chains.

We have tried to keep the size of square in proportion to the size of the quilt. For example, the wall quilt uses a 1" square, the baby quilt uses a 1-1/2" square, and the bed quilt uses a 2" square. Many antique Irish Chains are made with 2-1/2" and even 3" squares but we like the more intricate look of a smaller square. The *Triple* and *Quadruple* variations use a 1-1/2" square for the bed quilt because a bigger square would result in too large a block.

For better visual balance the quilts have an odd number of blocks, with chain blocks in the corners.

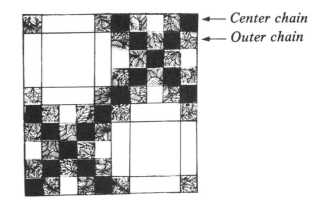

← Center chain
← Outer chain

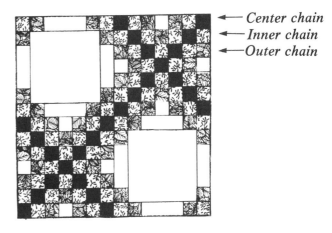

← Center chain
← Inner chain
← Outer chain

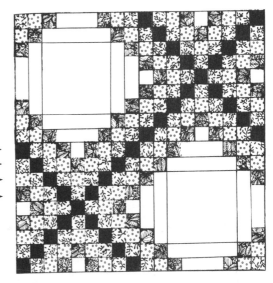
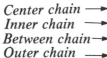

Center chain →
Inner chain →
Between chain →
Outer chain →

9

Making the Quilts

The *Irish Chain* quilt is an ideal pattern to use with streamlined cutting and sewing techniques. The fabrics are layered and cut into strips which are then sewn into groups. These groups are then cut apart and rearranged into the blocks.

The quilt has two basic blocks; a chain block of all small squares, and a background block which is a large square with smaller squares in the corners. When these blocks are set alternately together, they form the *Irish Chain* design.

The traditional background block was a large square with smaller squares appliqued in place in the corners. Our method requires piecing in the corner squares. If having seams in the background fabric is unacceptable to you, make the background blocks the traditional way.

Since the chain blocks have more seams than the background blocks, a slightly different seam allowance will result in the blocks being different sizes. It's best to cut and sew the chain blocks first, then cut and sew the background blocks to fit the chain blocks.

The *Double Irish Chain* quilt is made from narrow and wide strips of fabric. The *Triple* and *Quadruple* variations use narrow, medium and wide strips of fabric. Templates for these can be cut from a large sheet of posterboard. The templates sizes listed for each quilt include seam allowances. It is best if the templates are at least 18" long.

The grided rulers and plastic strips that are found in quilt shops and at quilt shows will also work.

Tracing around a posterboard or plastic strip will result in a slightly wider row than those marked with a grided ruler. This is not a problem unless traced strips are mixed with ruled strips.

Double Irish Chain

Chain block

Background block

Triple Irish Chain

Chain block

Background block

Quadruple Irish Chain

Chain block

Background block

Cutting

Each quilt lists the number of strips to cut from each fabric. The fabrics can be layered together to be cut or one fabric can be folded so several layers can be cut at a time.

Square the fabric by drawing a line perpendicular to the selvage. Trace the template, carefully overlapping to mark from selvage to selvage. Use a common line between rows. Divide the total number of strips needed by the number of layers of fabric to be cut to find how many rows to mark. For instance, if 11 strips are needed and the fabric is folded twice to form four layers, mark only 3 rows. This will yield 12 strips. Do not fold the fabric into more layers than can be cut accurately.

Fold the fabric without waste, trying to leave the leftover fabric in one piece. Try not to have the extra fabric draping off the table. Turn the piece around and leave all the extra fabric piled on the table where it will not be leaned on, which can distort the marking. Since folding does result in wasted fabric at each fold, we have allowed about 1/4 yard extra on all yardage amounts.

After pinning the layers together, cut the rows apart, keeping the scissors straight.

Most quilters using the rotary cutter prefer to fold their fabric in half lengthwise since they are limited by the size of the mats. Extra care should be given in placing the template at a right angle to the selvage. Otherwise the strips could be slightly V-shaped when unfolded. Usually it is not necessary to mark the strips when using the rotary cutter. A grided ruler or plastic strip measures the width of the rows. And since the fabrics are held down with the ruler during the cutting, no pinning is required.

These strips are then separated and arranged into different groups. Place the strips together and pin. Notice that the fabrics are different widths; avoid stretching them while sewing in an effort to make them even.

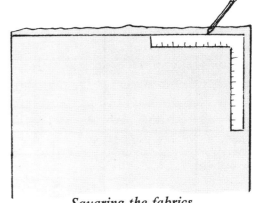

Squaring the fabrics

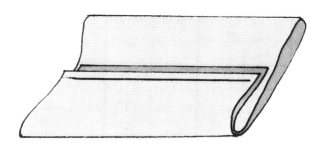

Folding the fabrics

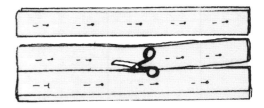

Cutting the strips

Sewing

A true 1/4" seam allowance is very important. The chain blocks contain more seams than the background blocks; too large a seam will result in a block too small, too small a seam will make a block that's bigger than the background block. That is why it is best to wait to cut the wider strips for the background blocks until a few of the chain blocks are made and measured.

Some sewing machines measure exactly 1/4" from the needle to the edge of the presser foot. Sometimes the needle can be adjusted further from or closer to the edge of the foot. A piece of masking tape on the throat plate of the machine can also serve as a guide. Sew a seam and measure it to determine whether it is correct.

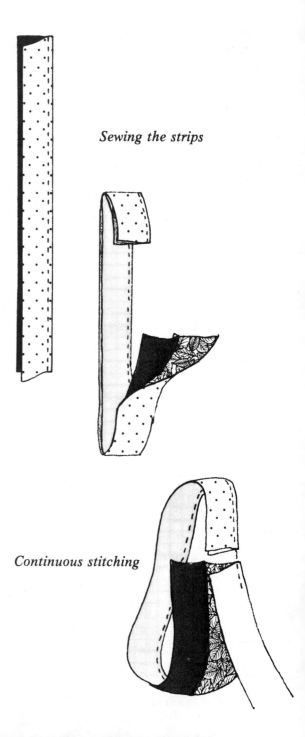

Sewing the strips

Sew the strips into the different arrangements or groups. These groups are identified by letters; beginning with the alphabet for the chain blocks, and the end of the alphabet for the background blocks.

Sew only one group at a time. They can be sewn with one continuous line of stitching. Simply bring the beginning edge of the strips around at the end of a seam. Without cutting the threads, open up the sewn strips and add the next one. After sewing a few inches, clip the thread holding the ends of the strips together. Each new strip is added to the right-hand edge.

Since these strips were cut on the crosswise grain of the fabric they have the ability to stretch. The sewing machine has a tendency to ease in the bottom layer of fabric and slightly drag or stretch the top layer. When this is combined with the habit of holding just the top strip, the results can be very uneven.

Continuous stitching

If each successive strip is pulled as it is sewn, the group will begin to ripple and curve. The first and last strip, of the *same* fabric, can even measure 2 or 3 inches differently. To prevent this from happening, simply smooth the bottom layer and place the top strip on it. Let the strips feed through the machine themselves, just guiding them enough to keep the seam consistent.

Pressing

The seams should be pressed in alternating directions and away from the background fabric. This will prevent shadowing since the background fabric is usually a lighter color and it will also help reinforce the illusion of the chains as foreground.

Beginning with Group A the seams will be pressed away from the background fabric. Notice that the seams will always be towards a certain fabric. This is a reminder of which direction to press, especially for groups that don't have any background strips.

Try not to stretch or curve the groups while pressing. Using a dry iron will also reduce distortion. After pressing from the back, turn and lightly press from the front.

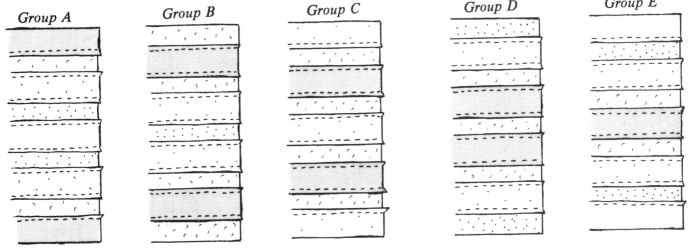

Double Irish Chain

Group A *Group B* *Group C*

Triple Irish Chain

Group A *Group B* *Group C* *Group D*

Quadruple Irish Chain

Group A *Group B* *Group C* *Group D* *Group E*

13

Cutting the Blocks

After the groups are pressed, place them face down. Using the narrow template or the grided ruler, mark and cut them into sections, beginning 1/2" away from the selvage. Always keep the template or ruler perpendicular to the seam lines. If the sections start looking crooked or slightly tilted, just skip over a space and start fresh.

The yardages were based on 40" of usable fabric in each group. The width of the fabric should yield the following number of sections:

1-1/2" sections — 27

1-3/4" sections — 23

2" sections — 20

2-1/2" sections — 16

It is possible to stack these groups and cut more than one at a time. This reduces the amount of marking. However, be extremely careful that the underneath layers are lined up exactly. There also will be quite a few layers at the seams which will be difficult to cut through. We usually stack only three or four groups.

After all the groups are cut into sections, separate by group.

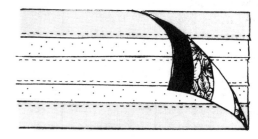

Stacking the groups

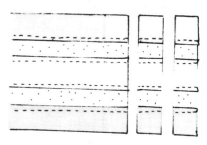

Cutting the sections

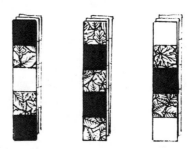

Stacking the sections

Sewing the Blocks

The cut sections should be placed in easy reach of the sewing machine. Take care to keep the 1/4" seam allowance consistent. When concentrating on matching the corners it is easy to ignore the seam allowance. By chain piecing these blocks it will be easier to keep a straight, consistent seam.

Begin by placing a section from Group A face up. Add a section from Group B. Match up the first corner, not the raw edges. Sew, matching up each corner. The alternate pressing sequence results in almost perfect piecing on the machine. Usually pinning isn't necessary since the corners can be held in place until they are sewn. However, on tiny squares such as the one inch in the wall quilt, there isn't much room to hold the fabric and pinning would be easier.

Without clipping the threads, sew the next A & B sections. Continue to do this for five to ten blocks. Without clipping the threads between the blocks, add the sections from Group C.

When the last of the needed sections are sewn, you will have completed blocks held together by the threads. Clip these apart to press.

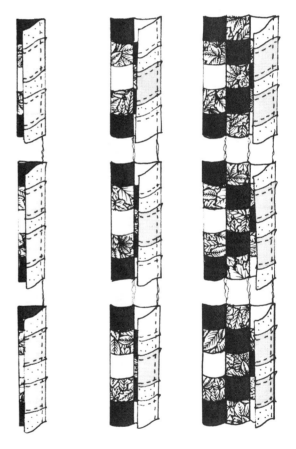

Sewing the blocks

Pressing the Blocks

The pressing sequence again alternates. Begin by pressing away from the background. It is easier to press these seams if the edge of the ironing board is used so the pressed seams can hang down out of the way.

A B C B A

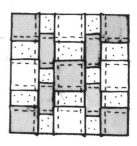

Double Irish Chain

A B C D C B A

Triple Irish Chain

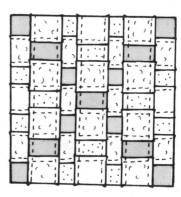

A B C D E D C B A

Quadruple Irish Chain

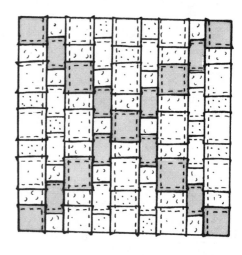

16

The Background Block

It is important to wait to *cut* the wider strips for the background block until the chain block is sewn and measured. The background block can then be made to fit the chain block. If the chain block was too small, the background strips could be trimmed. But if the chain block was too big, already cut strips would be too narrow. Measure the chain block before cutting the wider strips.

Measuring

Double Irish Chain—The wide strip should measure the same as the three inside squares of the chain block, plus seams.

Triple Irish Chain—The medium strip should measure the same as three inside squares, plus seams. The wide strip should measure the same as five inside squares, plus seams.

Quadruple Irish Chain—The medium strips should measure the same as three inside squares, plus seams. The wide strip should measure the same as five inside squares, plus seams.

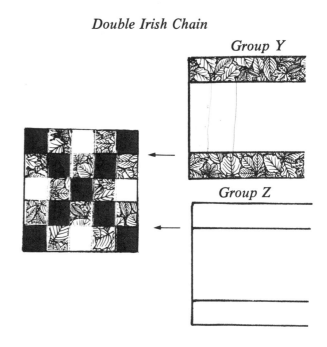

Double Irish Chain

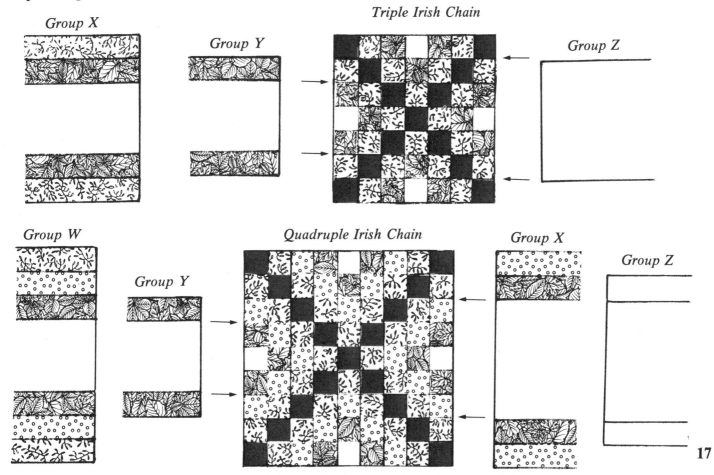

17

Sewing

Double Irish Chain—Sew the narrow and wide strips together for Groups Y & Z. The seams in Group Z will balance the other seams in the finished block. Press the seams in Group Y away from the wide strips and, in Group Z, towards the wide strip. Mark and cut Group Y into narrow sections the same width as the narrow strips. Mark and cut Group Z into wide sections the same width as the wide strips.

Sew two sections from Group Y to each wide section from Group Z to form the background block. These blocks can also be chain pieced. Press these seams towards the corner squares.

Triple Irish Chain—Sew the narrow and wide strips together to form Groups X and Y. Press the seams in alternate directions starting with them pressed away from the background fabric. Mark and cut them into narrow sections the same width as the narrow strips. Cut the wide strips into sections the same as the width. Sew two sections from Group Y to the top and bottom of the square. Then add two sections from Group X to the sides. Press these seams towards the corner squares.

Group Y
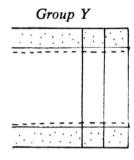

Group Z
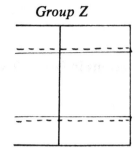

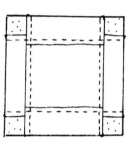

Y   Z   Y
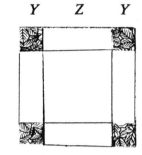

Group X

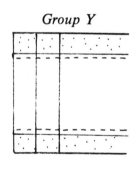

Group Y

Triple Irish Chain

Group Z
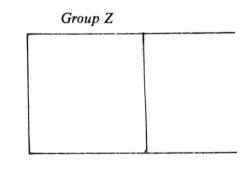

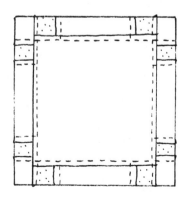

X   Y   X
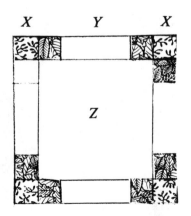

18

Quadruple Irish Chain—Sew the narrow, medium, and wide strips together to form Groups W, X, Y and Z. Press the seams in alternating directions, beginning by pressing away from the background fabric. The seams in Group Z will go towards the wide strip. Mark and cut Groups W, X and Y into narrow sections the same width as the narrow strips. Cut Group Z into wide sections measuring the same as the wide strip. Sew two sections from Group Y to the top and bottom of the wide sections. Sew two sections from Group X to the sides. Then sew two sections from Group W to the sides.

Press these seams in alternating directions, starting away from the center.

Group W *Group X*

Quadruple Irish Chain

Group Y *Group Z*

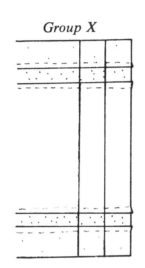
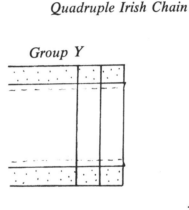
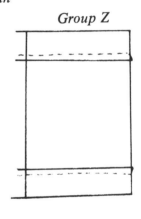

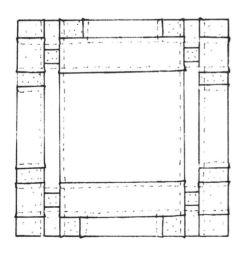
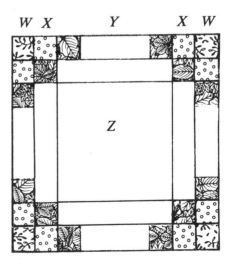

Joining the Blocks

Stack the finished blocks face down with the vertical seams parallel. It is important to have the blocks going the same direction. If some blocks are turned sideways it could be apparent from the print of the fabric. It will also be apparent from the way the blocks sew together. If they are placed correctly, the blocks will always be lengthwise to lengthwise grain and crosswise to crosswise grain. Since the crosswise grain has much more give than the lengthwise, this can make quite a difference in how the blocks sew together.

Chain piecing can also be used when joining the finished blocks. Place the chain blocks and the background blocks in stacks. Beginning with a chain block on the bottom and a background on top, sew, matching the corners. Without clipping the threads, sew two more blocks together, this time with the background block on the bottom. Continue sewing the first two blocks of all the rows. Without clipping the threads, add the third block to each row. Continue until all the blocks are joined into horizontal rows. Press these seams towards the background block.

The horizontal seams can be sewn with a minimum of pinning since the threads hold the rows together. Clip some of the threads on the larger quilts, making two or three sections since these will be easier to handle.

Chain piecing the rows

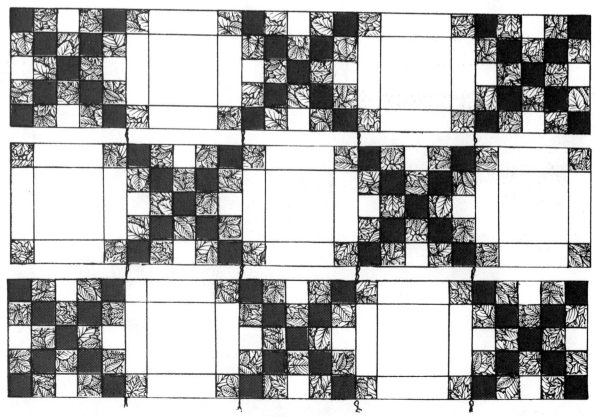

Patchwork Borders

A most elegant finish to these quilts is the patchwork border used on the quilts on the back cover and in plate 16. They were made with the same techniques used in making the quilt. The quilt and the patchwork border are edged with a plain border cut the same width as the narrow strips in the quilt. This could be any of the fabrics; however, the darkest tends to look the best.

After cutting the required number of strips, using the same template used for the narrow strips in the quilt, sew them into groups. This arrangement is the same as Group C in the *Double Irish Chain* and Group D in *Triple Irish Chain* and Group E in the *Quadruple Irish Chain*.

Press, alternating the direction of the seams and beginning with the seams away from the background fabric. Mark and cut them with the same template.

Sew them together, offsetting them one square. The chart lists how many sections needed for each border. These can be chain pieced by continuing the stitching to the raw edge of the fabric. Press the seams in alternate directions.

Double Irish Chain

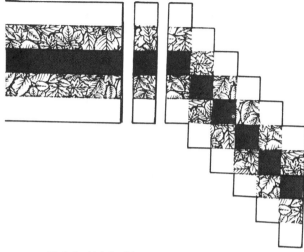

Triple Irish Chain

Quadruple Irish Chain

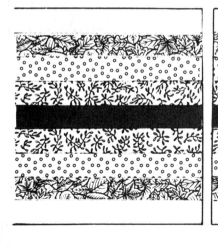

21

To complete each border it is necessary to piece one corner.

Double Irish Chain—Take two extra sections and remove the bottom square from one, and two squares from the other. These squares will complete the corner piece.

Triple Irish Chain—Take three extra sections and remove the bottom square from one section, two squares from the next, and three squares from the third section. When turned, these can be joined to form the corner.

Quadruple Irish Chain—Take four extra sections and remove the bottom square from one section, two squares from the next, three squares from the next, and four squares from the last section. When turned, these can be joined to form the corner.

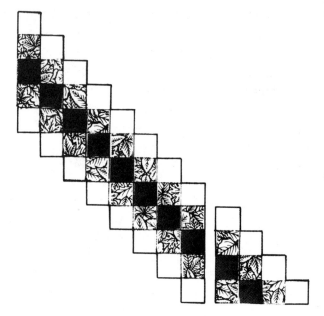

Forming the corners

Double Irish Chain

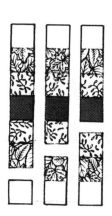 

Triple Irish Chain

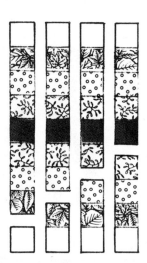 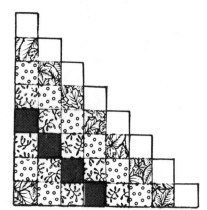

Quadruple Irish Chain

22

Measure the length of the patchwork border before joining them. Sometimes one more section is needed or one may need to be removed for the border to fit.

Join the four borders, with the top and bottom borders forming the corners. Sew the inside corner of the patchwork border to the corners of the quilt. The quilt should then be placed on a table for pinning. Since the edges of the patchwork border are on the bias, it is important not to stretch them while sewing, since this helps prevent distortion. The patchwork should always be the bottom layer during pinning and sewing. Finish sewing the borders to the sides of the quilt.

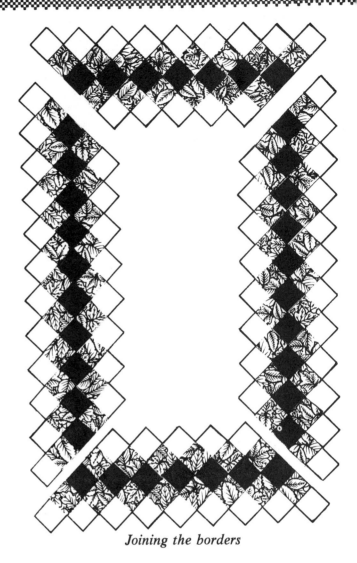

Joining the borders

Double Irish Chain Wall Quilt
Template size — 1-1/2″
Plain Borders — 1/2 yard

Fabric	Amount	Strips
Center chain	3/8 yard	5
Outer chain	5/8	10
Background	5/8	10

Sew 5 groups
    Top & bottom borders — 21 sections each
    Side borders — 19 sections each
    Border width (finished) — 2-3/4″

Double Irish Chain Wall Quilt
Template size — 1-3/4″
Plain borders — 3/4 yard

Fabric	Amount	Strips
Center chain	1/2 yard	5
Outer chain	3/4	10
Background	3/4	10

Sew 5 groups
    Top & bottom borders — 20 sections each
    Side borders — 18 sections each
    Border width (finished) — 3-1/2″

Double Irish Chain Baby Quilt
Template size — 2″
Plain Borders — 1 yard

Fabric	Amount	Strips
Center chain	1/2 yard	5
Outer chain	3/4	10
Background	3/4	10

Sew 5 groups
    Top & bottom borders — 20 sections each
    Side borders — 25 sections each
    Border width (finished) — 4-1/4″

Double Irish Chain Bed Quilt
Template size — 2-1/2"
Plain borders — 1-3/4 yards

Fabric	Amount	Strips
Center chain	3/4 yard	8
Outer chain	1 1/4	16
Background	1 1/4	16

Sew 8 groups
   Top & bottom borders — 27 sections
   Side borders — 32 sections
   Border width (finished) — 5-5/8"

Triple Irish Chain Baby Quilt
Template size — 1-3/4"
Plain borders — 1 yard

Fabric	Amount	Strips
Center chain	1/2 yard	6
Inner chain	3/4	12
Outer chain	3/4	12
Background	3/4	12

Sew 6 groups
   Top & bottom borders — 27 sections each
   Side borders — 36 sections each
   Border width (finished) — 5-1/4"

Quadruple Irish Chain Wall Quilt
Template size — 1-3/4"
Plain borders — 1 yard

Fabric	Amount	Strips
Center chain	3/8 yard	4
Inner chain	5/8	8
Between chain	5/8	8
Outer chain	5/8	8
Background	5/8	8

Sew 4 groups
   Top & bottom borders — 22 sections each
   Side borders — 20 sections each
   Border width (finished) — 7"

Triple Irish Chain Wall Quilt
Template size — 1-3/4"
Plain Borders — 1 yard

Fabric	Amount	Strips
Center chain	3/8 yard	5
Inner chain	3/4	10
Outer chain	3/4	10
Background	3/4	10

Sew 5 groups
   Top & bottom borders — 27 sections each
   Side borders — 25 sections each
   Border width (finished) — 5-1/4"

Triple Irish Chain Bed Quilt
Template size — 2"
Plain Borders — 1-3/4 yards

Fabric	Amount	Strips
Center chain	5/8 yard	9
Inner chain	1-1/8	18
Outer chain	1-1/8	18
Background	1-1/8	18

Sew 9 groups
   Top & bottom borders — 37 sections each
   Side borders — 45 sections each
   Border width (finished) — 6-3/8"

Quadruple Irish Chain Bed Quilt
Template size — 2"
Plain Borders — 1-3/4 yards

Fabric	Amount	Strips
Center chain	3/4 yard	9
Inner chain	1-1/4	18
Between chain	1-1/4	18
Outer chain	1-1/4	18
Background	1-1/4	18

Sew 9 groups
   Top & bottom borders — 34 sections each
   Side borders — 45 sections each
   Border width (finished) — 8-1/2"

1 *Shamrocks* (31'' x 31'') by Helen Young Frost.

2 Double Irish Chain quilt (70'' x 90'') by Debbie Gordon.

3 Double Irish Chain (38'' x 53'') by Eunice Mahony.

4 Double Irish Chain baby quilt (38" x 53") by Helen Young Frost; quilted by Beverly Packard.

5 Double Irish Chain quilt (50" x 90") by Sandee Streech.

6 Double Irish Chain quilt (47" x 62") by Dalene Thomas.

7 Triple Irish Chain quilt (76" x 97") by Louise Brown.

8 Triple Irish Chain quilt (81" x 103") by Pat Hunt.

9 Triple Irish Chain baby quilt (44' x 61") by Helen Young Frost; quilted by Lynette Bingham.

10 Double Irish Chain quilt (70" x 90") by Brenda Werbelow.

11 Double Irish Chain quilt (74" x 94") by Dalene Thomas.

12 Double Irish Chain quilt (80" x 100") by Blanche Young.

13 Quadruple Irish Chain wall quilt (41" x 41") by Debbie Gordon.

14 Double Irish Chain wall quilt (35" x 45") by Blanche Young.

15 *Irish Coffee* (42" x 42"), a quadruple variation by Blanche Young; quilted by Beverly Packard.

16 Double Irish Chain wall quilt (52" x 52") with patchwork border; by Helen Young Frost.

17 Triple Irish Chain by Ruth Gale.

18 Triple Irish Chain wall quilt (60" x 60") by Pam Cody.

19 Triple Irish Chain wall quilt (39" x 39") by Debbie Gordon.

20 Double Irish Chain quilt (52" x 67") by Mary Holmes.

21 Quadruple Irish Chain quilt (48" x 66") by Beth Kennedy.

22 Triple Irish Chain quilt (91" x 112") with patchwork border by Blanche Young.

23 *Red Delicious* (31" x 31") by Helen Young Frost; quilted by Lynette Bingham.

24 Triple Irish Chain quilt (95" x 116") by Dee Lynn.

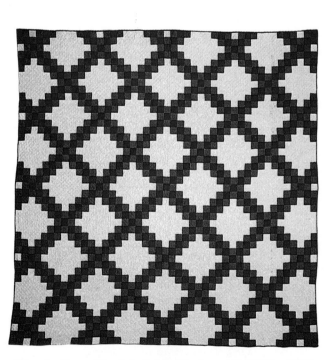

26 Antique Double Irish Chain quilt (90" x 90") circa 1850; from the collection of The Quilted Apple, Phoenix, Arizona.

25 Antique Double Irish Chain quilt (72" x 97") circa 1870; from the collection of Audrey Waite.

Borders

Borders not only give a quilt a beautiful frame, they will determine its finished size. Shown here are some border ideas. One way to design borders is to use the same size strips that were used in the quilt. They can even be placed in the same sequence.

The border for the wall and baby quilts should be cut across the width of the fabric, piecing if necessary. The yardage amounts listed with the wall and baby quilt allow for one complete border around the quilt. To use the same fabric twice, double the amount.

The borders for the bed quilts should be cut lengthwise on the fabric. The amounts listed will yield up to 5 inches of border from each fabric, piecing once on each side of the quilt. Wider borders or borders without piecing will require double the amount listed.

The quilts in plates 13 and 24 both have wonderful border variations that extend the design of the quilt into the border. Effects like this can be planned on graph paper.

Always measure for borders across the center of the quilt since the outside edges may have stretched. Mitered borders should be the size of the quilt plus twice the width of the borders, plus seams. When attaching a mitered border, be sure to start and stop the stitching 1/4" from the corner of the quilt. Fold back and crease the border, and then sew on the creased line.

Crease

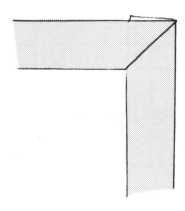

Mitered corners

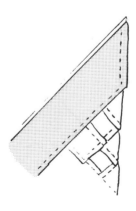

Border variations

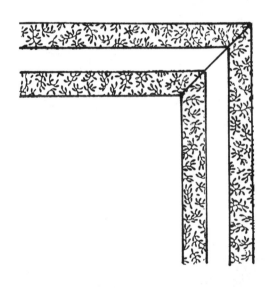

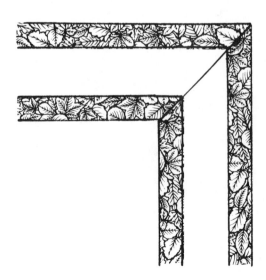

❖ Finishing the Quilts ❖❖❖❖❖❖❖❖❖

Quilting Ideas

The large background area provides a perfect opportunity to display a quilting design. We have offered several designs in the last pages. The same design can be used for different sizes of background blocks. It may be centered in the background block on the bed quilts, but extend into the chain blocks on the wall quilt. The designs can also be placed diagonally.

The chain blocks can be quilted straight, following the seams; diagonally through each square; diagonally, but spaced apart to avoid the bulk of the corner seams; or diagonally but offset to form a diamond in each square.

The quilting lines can extend to touch the central motif or they can frame the center design.

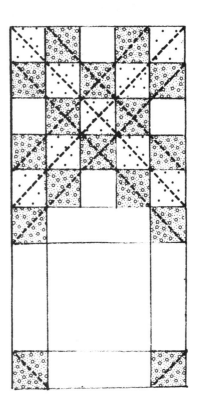

Quilting ideas

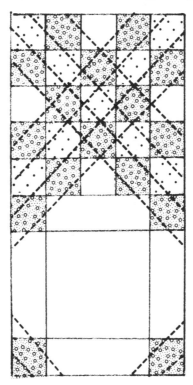

Marking for Quilting

Use a pencil or chalk pencil and a ruler to mark quilting lines on the squares. The center designs in the background blocks can be marked using a stencil, or tracing around a shape or by using a light box. Use a light touch when drawing the quilting lines in the background blocks.

The background blocks can be marked before they are joined to the chain blocks.

Basting the Quilt

Prepare the backing by sewing the lengths together with 3/4 inch seams. Press the seams open after trimming the selvages. Cut the backing and batting at least 2 inches larger than the quilt top on all sides. If the fabric is truly 45 inches wide, one length is all that is needed for the backing of the *Triple Irish Chain* wall and baby quilt. If it is too narrow, another length is needed, or the backing could be bordered with any of the extra fabrics.

Mark the center of each side of the backing, batting and quilt top. Spread the backing on a table or the floor. Carefully spread the batting, then the quilt on top, matching the center marks on the sides.

Baste, using a long needle and quilting thread, in rows every 6 to 8 inches, in both directions.

Quilting the Quilt

If the quilt is well basted, it is possible to begin quilting anywhere on the quilt. We have quilted all the background designs first, then the diagonal lines with good results.

Thread the needle with a single strand of quilting thread about 18 inches long. Begin and end each line of stitching by tying a single knot in the thread and popping it through the top layer into the batting. Try to have the stitches even and uniform.

Although traditionally only one color of thread was used, it is acceptable to use different colors of thread, matching the fabrics.

Binding the Quilt

To make a double layer bias binding, fold the cut edge of the fabric to the selvage. Fold again as shown. Measure and mark the first strip 2 inches from the folds. Continue marking strips every 4 inches. Cut on the marked lines. Join using 1/2 inch seams and trimming to 1/4 inch after pressing them open. Fold the binding in half lengthwise and press. Staystitch the edges together with a 1/4 inch seam. Leave the first 10 inches open.

Sew the binding to the three layers of the quilt. Stitch in 1/4 inch from the outside edge. Stop the stitching 1/4 inch away from the corners. Backstitch one stitch, then raise the needle and presser foot. Form a 1/2 inch pleat in the binding. Reinsert the needle on the other side of the pleat. Pivot the quilt and continue sewing.

Stop the stitching about 12 inches away from the starting point. Remove some of the staystitching and open the ends. Overlap the ends and mark, allowing for seams. Cut off the excess, then join the ends of the binding. Finish sewing the binding to the quilt. Trim the excess backing but leave an inch of batting to pad the binding. This will help it wear better. Blindstitch the binding to the back of the quilt.

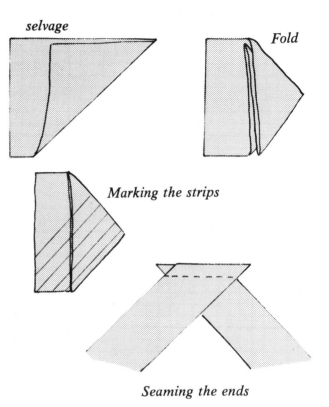

selvage

Fold

Marking the strips

Seaming the ends

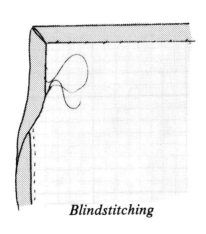

Blindstitching

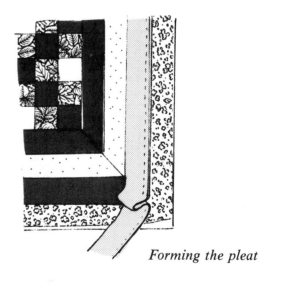

Forming the pleat

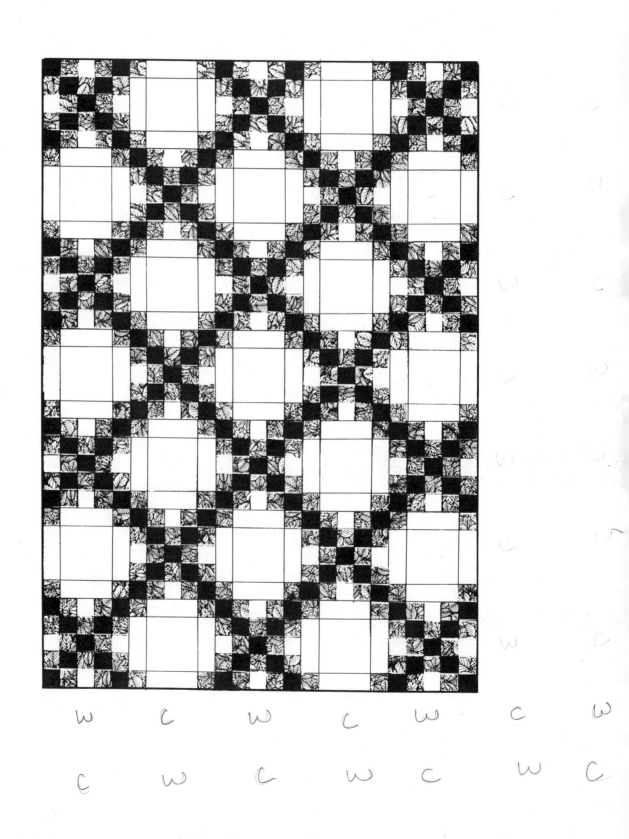

Each chain block consists of
2 sections from Group A
2 sections from Group B
1 section from Group C

Each background block consists of
2 sections from Group Y
1 section from Group Z

Group A

Group Y

Group B

Group Z

Group C

❖❖❖ Double Irish Chain ❖❖❖❖❖❖❖❖❖❖❖❖❖❖

Wall Quilt

Quilt size—25″ × 25″
Square size—1″
Block size—5″
Total blocks—25
Chain blocks—13   Template sizes
Background—12   Narrow—1-1/2″
                Wide—3-1/2″

Fabric	Amount	Strips to cut Narrow	Medium	Wide	Sew
Center chain	3/8 yard	5			Group A—1 Group Y—1
					Group B—1 Group Z—1
					Group C—1
Outer chains	5/8 yard	9			
Background	5/8 yard	5		2	Backing—1 yard
					Binding—3/4 yard
					Borders—1/4 yard for each 1″ of border.

Wall Quilt

Quilt size—31-1/4″ × 31-1/4″
Square size—1-1/4″
Block size—6-1/4″
Total blocks—25
Chain blocks—13   Template sizes
Background—12   Narrow—1-3/4″
                Wide—4-1/4″

Fabric	Amount	Strips to cut Narrow	Medium	Wide	Sew
Center chain	3/4 yard	9			Group A—2 Group Y—1
					Group B—2 Group Z—2
					Group C—1
Outer chain	1 yard	14			
Background	1-1/8 yards	8		3	Backing—1-1/4 yards
					Binding—1 yard
					Borders—3/8 yard for each 1-1/4″ of border.

Baby Quilt

Quilt size—37-1/2" × 52-1/2"
Square size—1-1/2"
Block size—7-1/2"
Total blocks—35
Chain blocks—18
Background—17

Template sizes
Narrow—2"
Wide—5"

Fabric	Amount	Strips to cut Narrow	Medium	Wide	Sew
Center chain	3/4 yard	9			Group A—2 Group Y—2
					Group B—2 Group Z—3
					Group C—1
Outer chains	1-1/4 yards	16			
					Backing—1-3/4 yards
					Binding—1 yard
Background	1-1/2 yards	10		5	Borders—3/4 yard for each 1-1/2" of border.

Bed Quilt

Quilt size—70" × 90"
Square size—2"
Block size—10"
Total blocks—63
Chain blocks—32
Background—31

Template sizes
Narrow—2-1/2"
Wide—6-1/2"

Fabric	Amount	Strips to cut Narrow	Medium	Wide	Sew
Center chain	1-3/4 yards	18			Group A—4 Group Y—4
					Group B—4 Group Z—6
					Group C—2
Outer chains	2-3/4 yards	32			
					Backing—6-1/2 yards
					Binding—1-1/2 yards
Background	3-3/4 yards	20		10	Borders—1-3/4 yards of 2 or 3 fabrics.

Triple Irish Chain

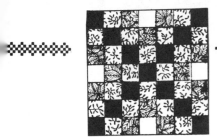 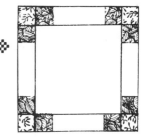

Each chain block consists of
2 sections from Group A
2 sections from Group B
2 sections from Group C
1 section from Group D

Each background block consists of
2 sections from Group X
2 sections from Group Y
1 section from Group Z

Group A

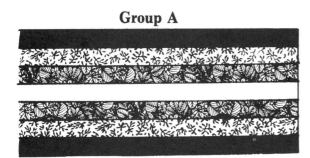

Group X

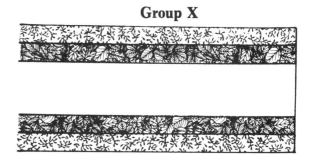

Group B

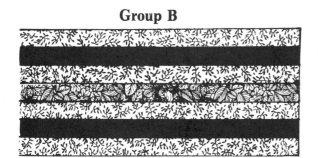

Group Y

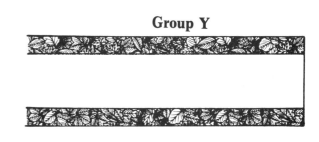

Group C

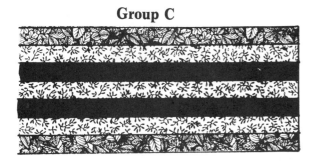

Group Z

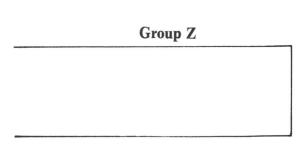

Group D

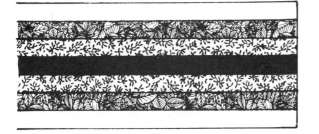

❖❖❖❖ Triple Irish Chain ❖❖❖❖❖❖❖❖❖❖❖
Wall Quilt

Quilt size—43-3/4″ × 43-3/4″
Square size—1-1/4″
Block size—8-3/4″
Total blocks—25
Chain blocks—13
Background—12

Template sizes
 Narrow—1-3/4″
 Medium—4-1/4″
 Wide—6-3/4″

Fabric		Amount	Strips to cut Narrow	Medium	Wide	Sew	
Center chain	■	1 yard	13			Group A—2	Group X—1
						Group B—2	Group Y—1
Inner chains	▦	1-1/2 yards	22			Group C—2	Group Z—2
						Group D—1	
Outer chains	▨	1 yard	16			Backing—2 yards	
						Binding—1-1/4 yard	
Background		1-1/4 yards	4	2	2	Borders—1/2 yard for each 1-1/4″ of border.	

Baby Quilt

Quilt size—43-3/4″ × 61-1/4″
Square size—1-1/4″
Block size—8-3/4″
Total blocks—35
Chain blocks—18
Background—17

Template sizes
 Narrow—1-3/4″
 Medium—4-1/4″
 Wide—6-3/4″

Fabric		Amount	Strips to cut Narrow	Medium	Wide	Sew	
Center chain	■	1 yard	13			Group A—2	Group X—2
						Group B—2	Group Y—2
Inner chains	▦	1-1/2 yards	24			Group C—2	Group Z—3
						Group D—1	
Outer chains	▨	1-1/4 yards	20			Backing— 3 yards	
						Binding—3/4 yard	
Background		1-3/4 yards	4	4	3	Borders—1/2 yard for each 1-1/4″ of border.	

Bed Quilt

Quilt size—73-1/2″ × 94-1/2″
Square size—1-1/2″
Block size—10-1/2″
Total blocks—63
Chain blocks—32
Background—31

Template sizes
Narrow—2″
Medium—5″
Wide—8″

Fabric	Amount	Narrow	Medium	Wide
		Strips to cut		
Center chain	2 yards	26		
Inner chains	3-1/4 yards	48		
Outer chains	2-3/4 yards	40		
Background	3-3/4 yards	8	8	7

Sew

Group A—4   Group X—4
Group B—4   Group Y—4
Group C—4   Group Z—7
Group D—2

Backing—6-1/2 yards
Binding—1-3/4 yards
Borders—1-3/4 yards of
     2 or 3 fabrics.

Quadruple Irish Chain

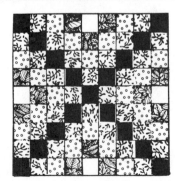

Each chain block consists of
  2 sections from Group A
  2 sections from Group B
  2 sections from Group C
  2 sections from Group D
  1 section from Group E

Each background block consists of
  2 sections from Group W
  2 sections from Group X
  2 sections from Group Y
  1 section from Group Z

46

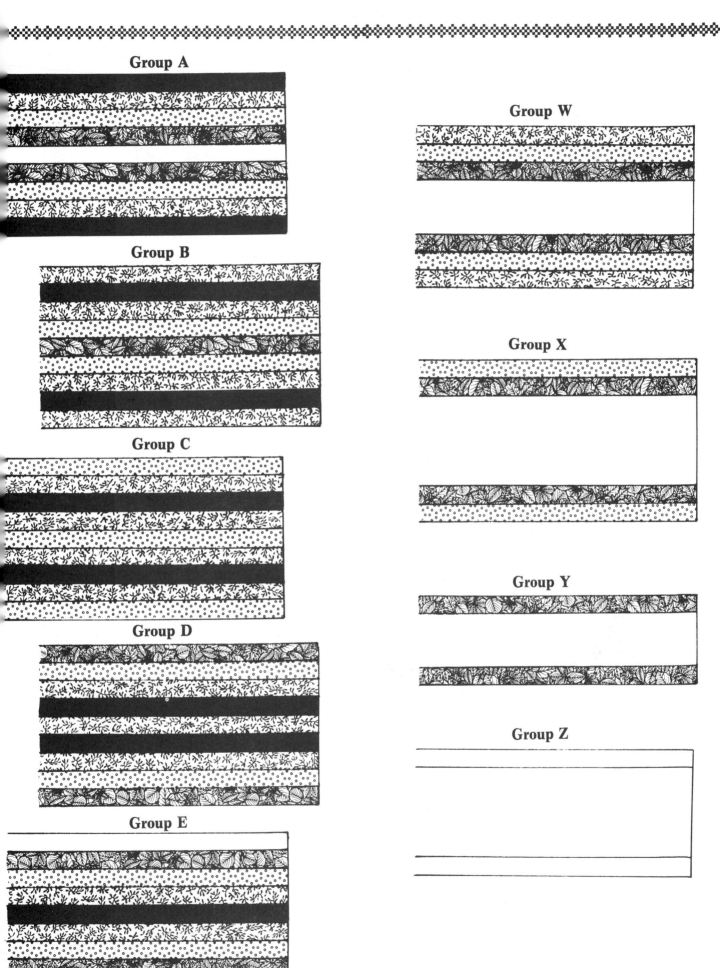

Group A

Group B

Group C

Group D

Group E

Group W

Group X

Group Y

Group Z

47

◆◆◆◆ Quadruple Irish Chain ◆◆◆◆◆◆◆◆
Wall Quilt

Quilt size—33-3/4" × 33-3/4"
Square size—1-1/4"
Block size—11-1/4"
Total blocks—9
Chain blocks—5
Background—4

Template sizes
   Narrow—1-3/4"
   Medium—4-1/4"
   Wide—6-3/4"

Fabric		Amount	Narrow	Medium	Wide	Sew
Center chain	■	3/4 yard	9			Group A—1 Group W—1
						Group B—1 Group X—1
Inner chains	▨	1 yard	17			Group C—1 Group Y—1
						Group D—1 Group Z—1
Between	▦	1 yard	15			Group E—1
Outer chains	▨	7/8 yard	13			Backing—1-1/4 yards
						Binding—1 yard
Background		1-1/4 yards	5	2	2	Borders—1/4 yard for each 1-1/4" of border.

Bed Quilt

Quilt size—67-1/2" × 94-1/2"
Square size—1-1/2"
Block size—13-1/2"
Total blocks—35
Chain blocks—18
Background—17

Template sizes
   Narrow—2"
   Medium—5"
   Wide—8"

Fabric		Amount	Narrow	Medium	Wide	Sew
Center chain	■	1-3/8 yards	17			Group A—2 Group W—2
						Group B—2 Group X—2
Inner chains	▨	2-1/4 yards	32			Group C—2 Group Y—2
						Group D—2 Group Z—4
Between chain	▦	2 yards	28			Group E—1
Outer chains	▨	1-3/4 yards	24			Backing—6-1/2 yards
						Binding—1-3/4 yards
						Borders—1-3/4 yards of 2 or 3 fabrics.
Background		3 yards	12	4	6	

48

Quilting Designs

Applique Designs

Make a pattern piece for every shape in the applique design. Trace around the pattern piece on the right side of the fabric with a pencil or chalk pencil. Cut out the shape allowing a scant 1/4" seam. Clip any inside corners or curves. The seam allowance can be basted under or simply turned under with the needle as the shape is appliqued.

Using a single strand of matching thread, applique each piece in place. Take small stitches, catching just the fold of the applique piece. Reinsert the needle into the background fabric directly in front of where the needle came out. Work on the edge facing you, using your thumb to hold the seam under as you applique.

Tracing the shape

Applique

56